- Successful Dating -

No More Frogs
Taurus

21 April – 20 May

by
Cathrine Dahl

CONTENTS

- Successful Dating -

No More Frogs

by Cathrine Dahl

No More Frogs - Successful Dating is your one-stop dating guide. No unnecessary blah-blah. The information is right here, at your fingertips.

This guide can be used in several ways. It's a handy tool when you want to prepare yourself a little. It can give you an advantage when going on a date or getting to know someone you've just met - or even someone you've known for a while.

Although this guide can help you angle your approach, remember to be true to yourself. Have fun, be wise, follow your heart - and keep your feet on the ground!

- Cathrine Dahl

Preface:
A few words about compatibility, and why compatibility guides can give you the wrong idea.

So you've met this Gemini you really, really like, but you're a Scorpio, and the compatibility guides say you're a lousy match. Guess what? That's rubbish!

Some compatibility guides offer a very simplistic approach, claiming that your best matches are the star signs within the same element as you:

Fire: Aries, Leo and Sagittarius
Earth: Taurus, Virgo and Capricorn
Air: Gemini, Libra and Aquarius
Water: Cancer, Scorpio and Pisces

Other guides are slightly more specific, declaring that we are compatible with star signs within our astrological polarity.

Yin: Taurus, Virgo, Capricorn, Cancer, Scorpio and Pisces
Yang: Aries, Leo, Sagittarius, Gemini, Libra and Aquarius

Doesn't look too good, does it? The most optimistic approach has removed half of the population from your dating pool. It doesn't make any sense. The true picture is far more promising...

One star sign, two very different personalities

Each of us has a unique astrological thumbprint determined by the sun, the moon and the planets. The most important factors being your ascending star (ascendant), the sun (star sign) and the moon (feelings).

Let's make it simple

Imagine your star sign being a melody. All the other aspects (the unique positioning of the moon and the planets) are sound effects, applied by a producer with a mixer.

The combination of rhythm, depth and base creates your unique sound. Another person with the same star sign will get his own sound mix and end up with a different beat.

Your personal melody can create wonderful harmonies with star signs you're not supposed to get on with – and nothing but noise with signs that are meant to be matches. You won't find out until you get to know each other.

Let's get to know your date...

THE MALE

YOUR DATE: TAURUS

21 April–20 May

The Essence of him

Handsome – masculine – charming – generous – affectionate – intelligent – stubborn – persistent – caring – loyal – classy – determined – stylish – a perfect gentleman when courting – has a strong sex-drive – traditional and a little conservative – intense – believe in the one big love – quality-conscious – goal-oriented – strong-willed – confident

...and remember: This guy can spot a fake immediately – both things and people. No matter what you do, be yourself and be genuine!

Blind Date – speedy essentials

Who's waiting for you?

There's no doubt about it: he's the stylish man with an aura of laid-back confidence who's sitting at the bar, idly swirling his drink around in his glass. He won't be obvious about it, but he'll regard you carefully before he decides to ask you to get a quick drink or treat you to dinner. He knows how to seduce women, but he can't be bothered by someone who's not up to his standards. Don't worry, he's far from arrogant – he just wants to be sure about you. This will save him – and you – from a broken heart later on.

Emergency fixes for embarrassing pauses

Be aware of any awkward moments of silence: they could be a sign that Mr Taurus is bored. He enjoys women who challenge him, provided it's not too much. Interesting questions, humorous comments and unusual points of view will sharpen his interest in you – but make sure you don't come across as a know-it-all.

Your place or mine?

This is no innocent little boy. His sex drive is strong. Although he's not seeking out casual relationships, he doesn't mind if a date night moves in a sensual direction. When and where? Doesn't really matter, as long as he feels comfortable and doesn't have to commit to breakfast.

Checklist, before you dash out to meet him:
Wear a classy detail (a watch, handbag, etc.)
(hint: no fakes)
Be up-to-date on the news
(hint: no celebrity gossip)
Look stylish and natural
(hint: no heavy perfume)
Arrive in the mood for something good to eat
(hint: no diets)
Be interesting and voice your opinions
(hint: but no fierce discussions)

Tip: Never rush this guy. Allow him to make up his mind – at his own pace. Push him, and he'll show you his stubborn side.

CHAPTER 1

PREPARE YOURSELF

Catch his eye, capture his attention
Top 10 attention grabbers

1. Admire his masculinity.
2. Wear something classy and sensual – and not too revealing.
3. Good body language and a relaxed posture.
4. Sparkling laugh and a positive personality.
5. A sensible and down-to-earth attitude.
6. Honesty is a must! Any evasiveness will leave him frustrated and impatient.
7. Make sure to have an open mind and don't be fixed in your views.
8. Let him know you've made an effort before seeing him – look good.
9. Intelligent comments and questions will cause him to pay attention.
10. Compliments work well, but only if they are sincere. He will quickly call your bluff.

The SHE. The woman!

Although a Taurus man may fall for a pretty face and a sleek body, inner beauty is just as important to him – probably even more so. However, this doesn't mean that his ideal woman will ever let herself go. Looks are important to him – but they're not the only thing. Superficial women have no room in his life. His partner must be a little bit of everything: soft, feminine, independent, strong, loyal and intelligent, with a well-developed sense of humour. He needs someone he can trust and rely on, not a social butterfly or a bar-babe.

The Essence of her
Smart – compassionate – fit, with a healthy outlook on life – intelligent – independent – loyal and supportive – sensual – strong – feminine – has a good sense of humour – grounded – classy – appreciative of family life – assertive in her professional life – appreciates the finer things – a good hostess – charming in social settings – a reliable team player – passionate and romantic

---

Taurus arousal meter
From 0 to 100... In five seconds – or two hours! There are no rules. This man is either-or. But with the right encouragement, his erotic intensity may sparkle like a firework.

Remember: Be true to yourself

It doesn't matter if he is the most stunning guy you've ever met – if you don't match, you don't match. You may be able to put on a show for a while to hold his attention, but what's the point? We can't please everybody. We all have different needs, dreams, tastes and preferences. There's no such thing as a one-size-fits-all lover. Be yourself, and be true to who you are – always!

Very important: Never tease him or play hard to get. If you hint at one thing but do the opposite, you'll just end up confusing him – and losing him.

CHAPTER 2

THE FIRST DATE

Getting your foot in the door
The basics

No aggressiveness, please. Don't throw yourself at him. Guide him gently with hints and suggestive glances, but don't be too obvious about your interest. If he finds you interesting, he will connect the dots very quickly.

The beauty within. He appreciates style and physical looks, but inner beauty is just as important.

Keep it discreet. A small touch of luxury can be attractive, but don't overdo it. You don't want to come across as someone who throws money around.

Never fake it. Don't wear fake designer goods and pretend they are real. He has no room for fakes in his life – whether things or people.

No negative stuff. Keep the conversation bright, positive and optimistic. Talking about depressing stuff in the news will give him a headache.

Intelligent flattery. If you can draw positive attention to something about him that isn't obvious, you will score points.

Whatever you do...

- **DON'T** become overly engaged during discussions.

- **DON'T** make promises you can't keep. He won't forget.

- **DON'T** wear too much perfume or makeup. Keep it natural.

- **DON'T** try to impress him with fake bling.

- **DON'T** take his generosity for granted.

Remember,

Take the initiative and show interest. If he pampers you without getting anything in

• **DON'T** rush him – about anything.

• **DON'T** lie – not even little white lies.

• **DON'T** be secretive. Evasiveness annoys him endlessly.

• **DON'T** be picky about food or fuss about being on a diet.

• **DON'T** express your feelings with subtle hints. He'll either

get it wrong or not notice at all.

return, he's liable to lose interest and disappear.

Signs you're in - or not

The Taurus man is an either-or kind of guy: he's either interested or he's not. The specific kind of interest, however, depends on your first date. If you had a hot and erotic date, it could be that he's simply looking for more of the same. If sex hasn't entered the picture but the two of you got on really well, there are foolproof signals that you have sparked his interest. There's no need to interpret anything. There are no hidden messages. This guy is blunt and straightforward. Look out for the following:

Chances are he will...

- call you as soon as he gets a chance
- suggest seeing you again as soon as possible
- pay you compliments and show an interest in what you're doing
- give you a little something to show that he cares
- act playfully jealous of other men (he might actually be a little jealous)
- make an effort to impress you: a homemade meal, a special drink, a reservation somewhere nice...

Not your type? Making an exit

Leaving a Taurus man can be a challenge – it depends how hooked he is. Although he may have a casual attitude toward sex, he seldom drifts from one romantic relationship to another. If he has decided to spend time and energy on you, he's doing it for a reason –he likes you. When a man born under the sign of Taurus makes up his mind, he is prepared to apply his patience and persistence to making things work – even if you think it's pointless...

However, there are limits to how far Mr Taurus is willing to go – how much rubbish he is willing to tolerate, and how much stupidity he can live with every day. Take it upon yourself to look bad, and the exit ought to be smooth and quick.

Foolproof exit measures:

Think twice before trying out any of the suggestions below. Besides making you look bad, some are downright mean.

- No more sex! Blame whatever. Headaches. Work. The colour of his socks.
- Criticise his sex drive and tell him to cool down.
- Turn everything into a discussion: big issues, tiny details, anything.
- Insist that he go on a diet.
- Spend money on fake designer items, and claim you thought they were real.
- Tell him to hurry up, no matter what he's doing

CHAPTER 3

SEX'N STUFF

Seductive moves:
How to get him in the mood:

Never be impatient with this guy. You can nudge him carefully, but never, ever push him. Luckily, when it comes to sex, you probably won't have to. If he doesn't respond to your erotic invitation, he's probably knocked out with the flu.

Preferences and erotic nature

Sex is important to a Taurus man on many levels. It's a source of energy, inspiration and relaxation – as well as a potent confirmation of his masculinity (not that he needs any confirmation ... you're dealing with is a confident guy). This masculine approach leaves a lot up to him, and he enjoys taking the initiative and being in charge. However, he feeds on feedback from his partner! This is important. For him, there is no such thing as sex without pleasing his partner, and he wants to be sure he's doing just that. A seemingly indifferent woman – even just a quiet woman – can turn him off completely.

Hitting the right buttons

Although every sign has areas that are more sensitive than others, individual sensitivity may vary quite a bit. Don't go body-blind. Honing in on these erogenous zones and forgetting the rest of him is not a good idea. Use his erogenous zones to create sparks while turning him on, and as a passion booster when it gets heated. Watch his body language – including the most obvious of signs! Open your mind to the sensuality of touch and taste.

Key areas
His throat and neck

Get it on
You can spark his interest anytime, anywhere, without making it obvious to the people around you! The sensitivity of his throat and the neck provide endless opportunities to 'accidentally' heat him up. If you're out in public, be casual about it. Make him wonder about your intentions.

Arouse him
Carefully touch him while adjusting his sweater, tie or jacket. Allow the tips of your fingers to gently brush against the back of his neck while sitting next to him on a bus or in a taxi. And obviously: soft lips or the tip of your tongue gently playing along his throat during sex will act as a nice passion-booster.

Surprise him

When it comes to sex, he's pretty much ready anytime, and on short notice. But with a little creativity, it's still possible to surprise him. Suggest an erotic encounter in an unusual place when he least expects it. Big bonus if you're by yourselves, surrounded by nature...

Spice it up

He is a very sensual being, and you can play to this. Try adding an element of taste during foreplay, like whipped cream or chocolate. For smell, pleasant – and lightly scented! – aromatic oils are perfect for a sensual massage.

Remember: He doesn't really need reassurance, but he appreciates a partner who recognizes him as a wonderful and passionate lover. Be vocal.

His expectations

Be ready. He expects a woman to be sensually spontaneous and play along when the erotic temperature is on the rise.

Embrace his passion. A woman who doesn't enjoy an erotic man, should go looking for someone else. The Taurus male needs a woman who appreciates his passion. Too many rejections will turn him off his partner.

No hard core! Although he does have a liberal streak, he does not appreciate anything vulgar in bed.

Femininity rules! His partner needs to be tender, sensual and passionate. Wearing feminine and slightly sassy underwear is a nice touch.

Participate. A passive partner is a major turn off. She must actively participate and let him know clearly that she appreciates what he's doing.

Sensuality. He uses his senses actively during sex, and he enjoys the natural scents of a woman – not a body showered with perfume. Strong artificial smells can ruin the overall experience for him.

Your sensual preferences
Quiz yourself and find out whether this man is for you.

Where on the scale are you?
1 = Don't agree | 3 = Sure | 5 = Agree!

1. Expressing passion is very important during sex.
One a scale for 1 to 5, you are : 1 - 2 - 3- 4 - 5

2. Having sex in new places can add erotic dimensions.
One a scale for 1 to 5, you are : 1 - 2 - 3- 4 - 5

3. Frequent sex is important in order to thrive.
One a scale for 1 to 5, you are : 1 - 2 - 3- 4 - 5

4. Too much romantic sensitivity ruins the excitement of sex.
One a scale for 1 to 5, you are : 1 - 2 - 3- 4 - 5

Score 15–20: Hot and steamy. Spontaneous and exciting. Never, ever boring!
Score 10–14: He may be a bit much at times, but you're probably up for it!
Score 5–9: Let him know what pleases you. Guide him, but don't criticise.
Score 1–4: You may feel overwhelmed by this guy. Make sure to tell him about your preferences before jumping into bed.

CHAPTER 4

GENERAL STUFF

The big picture

Keep in mind that the characteristics of a Taurus may vary quite a bit depending on where within the sign he was born, as well as a wide range of additional astrological factors. But for now, let's stick to the basics. Just remember: don't jump to conclusions as soon as you meet him. Give him room to shine. Get to know the man behind the sign.

His personality: Pros and cons

Pros	Cons
• Loyal and supportive	• Stubborn
• Romantic	• Slow
• Kind	• Rigid
• Masculine	• Lazy
• Passionate	• Dwells on the past
• Persistent and assertive	• Possessive
• Humorous	• Pushy
• Determined	• Ignorant
• Has an eye for quality	• Arrogant
• Confident	• A womaniser
• Enjoys the good things in life	• Argumentative
• Charming	• Patronizing
• Frank	• Demanding
• Erotic	• Critical
• Down-to-earth	• Has a low tolerance for criticism

Tip: How to show romantic interest

Taking interest in what he's doing is a good start. Making an effort to do something nice, like preparing dinner or giving him a gift that's a little out of the ordinary, will make him realise he's got something good going on...

Romantic Vibes

Mr Taurus:
The romantic and attentive partner

The essence

The knight in shining armour. He can be a real chivalrous gentleman. In his mind, he sometimes sees himself as a knight, looking for a princess to rescue. In the real world, he's still a man – but he's quite a catch, and he knows it.

Choosy. Don't think you've captured this guy just because you've had one hot date. Sex and love are two different things for this man, and he's choosier about who he lets into his heart than who he lets into his bedroom.

Pamper his woman. If you have managed to capture his romantic attention, you have a lot to look forward to. He will treat you like a princess, spoiling you with little gifts and loads of tender attention.

Showing you off. The moment he's your guy, he won't hesitate to show you off to the world. He will be proud of you.

Intimacy is important. He is a romantic with a fondness for the intimacy he can create when he's alone with his partner. And he's is open to suggestions!

Knows his stuff. Mr Taurus is kind, loyal, intense, passionate – and stubborn. He's also an extremely charming man who knows how to take care of his woman.

Tip: How to show erotic interest

That's easy. A glance, a smile, a sweet comment... His erotic antennas are finely tuned, and he will pick up on erotic interest right away. He doesn't get coy flirtation. Either you want to have sex, or you don't.

Erotic Vibrations

Mr Taurus:
The passionate and determined lover

The essence

When he's hot, he's hot! Don't expect him to be a sweet and sensitive lover who holds back his own desires to wait for the right moment. As soon as you have sparked his passion, he's ready to go...

If you start something, finish it. If you don't want to have sex, don't tease him. If you do, you can wave goodbye to future dates.

Be genuine. Mr Taurus expects people to be genuine on all fronts. Saying one thing and doing something different does not go down well with him – in any area of life!

Strong sex drive. He's usually patient, but not when it comes to sex. His sex drive is strong. If he could work out in bed rather that at the gym, he'd probably do it.

Don't make it complicated. More sensitive guys may be inclined to use sex to communicate feelings and tenderness with their partners. Not this guy. He appreciates sex for its own sake.

His partner is queen! He doesn't get pleasure from sex unless his partner enjoys it as much as he does. His number one is to make sure she is happy.

CHAPTER 5

COMPATIBILITY QUIZ

Are you banging your head against the wall, or does he unleash your positive potential? Do you provoke him or bring out the best in him? Does he make you throw your arms up in exasperation, or do you feel inspired and complete in his company? Are the two of you headed towards doom or dream? Take the test to find out.

Question 1.
How would you feel about a guy who made erotic advances when you least expected it?

A. Not really my thing. I don't like sexually intense guys.
B. That would depend on my mood. I guess it could be fun...
C. I'd love it! I love spontaneity, excitement and never knowing when it's going to happen.

Question 2.
Do you enjoy good food?

A. Food itself is no big deal. A nice atmosphere and good company are far more important.
B. Food is fuel. I don't understand why people make such a fuss about it.
C. I love cooking – bringing out new flavours, trying new things.

(cont.)

Question 3.
As a lover, which of these keywords fits you the best?

A. Playful and active.
B. Intense and passionate.
C. Passive and conservative.

Question 4.
Which of these keywords fits your ideal partner?

A. Grounded, intense, masculine.
B. Determined, creative, adventurous.
C. Dreamy, romantic, sensitive.

Question 5.
Do you think it's important to support and encourage your partner when the world turns against him?

A. Of course! Everyone needs a supportive partner.
B. Well, I try to do that ... but he doesn't seem to need it.
C. No need. The man in my life is strong and capable of taking care of himself.

Question 6.
What's the first thing that springs to mind when you see the words 'whipped cream'?

A. A big dessert with loads of calories?
B. A very sensual evening...
C. Fun, games, mess and laughter

Question 7.
How do you tend to show your love for your partner?

A. I tell him how I feel.
B. I usually pamper him a little: buy him a gift or give him a massage.
C. He knows I love him. No need to rattle on about it all the time.

Question 8.
You've decided to get some work done. How do you respond when your partner lights a candle, opens a bottle of wine and gives you a suggestive look?

A. It would really annoy me, especially if he knew I had work to do.
B. I expect that he'd manage to persuade me to take a break.
C. I'd love it. This is one of the things that make my partner so special.

Question 9.
Do you think it's important to show affection in bed?

A. I prefer hot passion that leaves little room for tenderness and affection.
B. Of course. Sex without affection is cold and impersonal.
C. It depends. Sometimes things are passionate and steamy; other times it's close, sweet and affectionate.

Question 10
Do you ever take the initiative to spice things up in the bedroom?

A. Yes, often. My partner seems to appreciate the initiative.
B. Never. I don't regard myself as sexually aggressive.
C. Sometimes, but it's never anything too extreme.

SCORE	A	B	C
Question 1	1	5	10
Question 2	5	1	10
Question 3	5	10	1
Question 4	10	5	1
Question 5	10	5	1
Question 6	1	10	5
Question 7	5	10	1
Question 8	1	5	10
Question 9	1	5	10
Question 10	10	1	5

75 – 100
This is a perfect match, but you probably knew that already. You may be quite different, but both of your fundamental values are strong. It's almost as if you share a subconscious understanding, and all it takes to communicate is a look and a smile. Exploring life's pleasures is important: art, food, sex... The ability to discover joy and adventure in the smallest of things makes this relationship happy, exciting and unique.

51 – 74
From simple bliss to exciting challenges, this relationship will never be boring. You may provoke each other at times, but you never seem to cross the line. Instead of getting on each other's nerves, you inspire one another and bring energy to the relationship. Your differences may make you stronger as individuals, but they will bring you closer as a couple. Flexibility and patience are important for making this relationship flourish – but you knew that already. Take time seize the moment and embrace the pleasures. It will bring a wonderful dimension to the relationship.

26 – 50

One thing is certain: this relationship will never be boring. Some people love intense energy ... but it takes two to tango. If one of you finds it difficult to keep up with the other, the whole thing can become draining. Or it could be that you both apply your energy to different areas of your life – the same problem will arise. In order for this to work, you'll need to figure out whether you're able to channel your energy in the same direction. If you manage to find a common ground, you'll still need to be honest with each other – and true to yourselves. Love is a powerful thing, but if you feel there's more nagging than hugging going on here, it might be better to opt for a close and strong friendship.

10 – 25

It may have been fun at first. It may even have been passionate and exciting. But how do you feel now? Certain experiences in life are meant to be passing. This adventure may be one of them. Embrace the excitement of a new experience, and leave it at that. True harmony and lasting romantic love will be found elsewhere. Life is for living, and we need to surround ourselves with people who bring out the best in us. Start looking...

Suggestion

Never hold on to something just for the sake of it. Make sure there is a good reason for what you do - and that whatever you do brings you happiness.

THE FEMALE

YOUR DATE: TAURUS

21 April–20 May

The Essence of her

Charming – feminine – determined – wise – self-disciplined – confident and strong, but longs for a masculine man – quality-conscious, both about people and things – reliable and responsible – loyal – sensual and romantic – sensitive to atmosphere – generous and kind – genuine and honest – hard-working – realistic – down-to-earth – has a fondness for beauty

...and remember: She is friendly and open, but she won't reveal too much right away. She prefers to get to know people before she opens up.

Blind Date – speedy essentials

Who's waiting for you?

If she has to wait for you, she will probably keep looking at her watch and glancing towards the door. She'll hate to think that you've stood her up. However, if she's early and has some time to kill, she might just browse through a magazine while sipping a drink. She won't mind; she enjoys her own company. She will be stylish, feminine and attractive. You'll notice something playful in her eyes, but you'll soon discover that she's saving a lot for later. What you're getting is a preview.

Emergency fixes for embarrassing pauses.

With a Taurus woman, pauses are warning signals – and a cue for you to get your act together. She is far too polite to allow a conversation to be stuck for long. But if she starts glancing across the room, she might be thinking 'What am I doing here?' If you like her, mention something interesting or fun you've done: taken a DJ gig for a local jazz station, written a book or an article, trekked through wilderness or even just cooked something impressive ... but whatever it is, be modest about it.

Your place or mine?

If you find yourself in bed with her on the first date, then you must have made a profound impression. In fact, you must be close to her vision of the perfect guy. She seldom has casual sex – not because she's a prude, but because she doesn't get any real satisfaction from sex with a man she doesn't know. Sure, a little fun is OK, but a one-night stand is usually more hassle than anything.

Checklist, before you dash out to meet her:

Be on time

(hint: never make her doubt you)

Send a quick text beforehand, confirming the date

(hint: she appreciates the small details)

Wear a nice outfit, but nothing over the top

(hint: casual masculinity will do)

Be well groomed, but with no – or very little – cologne

(hint: keep it clean and natural)

Have some info about the menu or the place

(hint: be prepared)

Tip: She is sensual, independent, confident – and strong enough to be weak. When she finds the right man, she will allow him to become the king of her life.

CHAPTER 1

PREPARE YOURSELF

Catch her eye, capture her attention
Top 10 attention grabbers

1. Show your strong and masculine side.
2. Make sure your comments are smart and often humorous.
3. There's no need to be a free spender when you're out, but be generous.
4. A personal gift that shows you have paid attention will go a long way.
5. Give her your complete attention. No distracting glances at other women.
6. Ask her to call you to let you know that she's home safely.
7. Be stylish and elegant – no matter what you're wearing.
8. Show support and enthusiasm for her projects and ideas.
9. Be compassionate and considerate.
10. Sport a little luxury, but no bling.

The HE. The man!

The Taurus woman prefers cool cats, not kittens. You won't find her obsessing over a cute butt. She appreciates the features of a man that reflect his strength, like arms and shoulders. She respects a man's integrity and will prioritise personal qualities over looks. However, if she can, she'd like to have both.

The Essence of him
Attentive– intelligent – down-to-earth – playful, enthusiastic and creative – has a fondness for comfortable luxuries – sensitive to beautiful and sensual – has an alert mind – enjoys the arts, music and exquisite food – confident– compassionate – loyal and trustworthy – sensual and erotic – strong and fit

Taurus arousal meter
From 0 to 100... In an hour or two. She normally needs time to get into the mood. However, visual stimulation can speed things up considerably. Try a very innocent erotic move – no porn!

Remember: Be true to yourself

It doesn't matter if she is the most stunning girl you've ever met – if you don't match, you don't match. You may be able to put on a show for a while to hold her attention, but what's the point? We can't please everybody. We all have different needs, dreams, tastes and preferences. There's no such thing as a one-size-fits-all lover. Be yourself, and be true to who you are – always!

Very important: A cheap present will be regarded as an insult – unless there's a personal story behind it.

CHAPTER 2

THE FIRST DATE

Getting your foot in the door
The basics

No cheap hook-up lines. 'Hey babe, fancy a bit of man' is definitely not the right approach. This is a feminine, sensual, classy and romantic woman, and cheap remarks will get you nowhere. In fact, if you want to seduce her, you'll need to avoid anything cheap.

Polish your manners. The Taurus woman expects to be treated gallantly, so polish up your manners and put your best foot forward. Be attentive and polite.

Let's go out. Invite her out, but not to a place that offers juicy discounts and supersaver quarter-pound burgers. If you suggest this, she'll probably think you're joking. If you can't afford to splash out on a fancy meal, be clever about it: invite her on a picnic in a scenic place.

Be attentive. The Taurus woman loves receiving compliments and small tokens of affection: a sweet comment, a kiss on the cheek, a hug, an unexpected text or phone call, a little gift.

Never take her for granted. Make sure she feels valued, respected and appreciated.

Whatever you do...

- **DON'T** be pushy. Allow her to make up her mind.

- **DON'T** be cheap.

- **DON'T** give her any reason to doubt you. Be reliable.

- **DON'T** be careless about your appearance.

- **DON'T** show off or brag about yourself.

Remember,
She can be very slow about showing her interest, and she may need a nudge once in a

- **DON'T** be too extravagant. She may start worrying about

making it up to you.

- **DON'T** flirt with other women, no matter how innocently.

- **DON'T** take her attention and generosity for granted.

- **DON'T** get into petty arguments. Handle situations with dignity.

- **DON'T** pretend to be interested if you're not.

while. If you haven't heard from her, send her a text.

Signs you're in - or not

When courting a Taurus woman, there are two things to keep in mind: 1) she's a slow mover; 2) she's not great with hints. Be straight with her. The challenge is to deliver straightforwardness in a gentle manner. A man who suddenly declares his love after casual, friendly interactions will freak her out! However, she does appreciate persistent men – provided they are classy about it. This makes her feel desired and gives her time to make up her mind. But even when she's decided she's interested, she can be surprisingly reserved, especially considering how assertive she is in her professional life. However, if she really likes you and feels comfortable around you, she may give you a few hints:

Chances are she will...

- show genuine interest in you and pay you compliments
- give you a gift – a very nice gift
- offer to do something for you
- pamper you with attention and maybe a massage. She will call and text you
- be protective of you

Not your type? Making an exit

The Taurus woman is the most loyal woman in the zodiac. She is also extremely protective. If someone were to touch a hair on her man's head, they'd be sorry – very sorry. Like a raging bull or a fierce mama bear, she will take on anyone to protect the people she loves. Her relationships are precious, and that's why she waits a long time before committing herself to a partnership. Her loyalty is too valuable to waste on someone who's not worth it.

But sometimes, she gets too comfortable. Sometimes, she fails to see that life has more to offer, and she sticks around ... and sticks around ... and sticks around. Breaking up with her isn't easy, especially because her romantic relationships have a tendency to turn into friendships – and who would break up with a friend?

Foolproof exit measures:

If you're tired of being her buddy and miss being somebody's hot lover, there are a few options to help you move on. Some examples include the following:

- Stand her up, and offer feeble excuses for why you didn't show
- Push her into making decisions about the future
- Criticise her work ethics, her morals and her commitment
- Be demanding and ungrateful
- Be rude and inconsiderate towards others
- Criticise her friends and family
- Flirt with other women, both online and in the real world

CHAPTER 3

SEX'N STUFF

Seductive moves:
How to get her in the mood:

The Taurus woman is not particularly impulsive, so erotic surprises are not her thing. Take your time to get her in the mood. As soon as she gets going, she'll keep going. Either way, there will be no quick mood changes – unless you watch an erotic movie together. Her sex life is passionate and precious, and she shouldn't be rushed.

Preferences and erotic nature

She appreciates a real and genuine man – no fakes or wannabes. She is most easily turned on by a muscular and strong body. However, if the man has an erotic mindset and sensual personality, then his looks are less important. She loves being kissed and touched all over, as well as having seductive suggestions whispered in to her ear. She appreciates clean, natural scents. Cologne can turn her off in bed. She needs to take her time, and she expects her lover to respect that. He needs to be sensitive and assertive at the same time.

Hitting the right buttons

Although every sign has areas on the body that are more sensitive than others, individual sensitivity may vary quite a bit. Don't go body-blind. Honing in on these erogenous zones and forgetting the rest of her is not a good idea. Use these areas to create sparks while turning her on, and as a passion-booster when things get heated. Watch her body language – including the most obvious of signs. Open your mind to the sensuality of touch and taste.

Key area
Her neck and throat

Get it on
The slightest touch on her neck can send goosebumps all the way down to her toes. The move may seem innocent, but this region of her body is a very powerful 'on' button. It's a convenient erogenous zone for stimulating her both privately and in public.

Arouse her
If you have just met her, you can 'accidentally' touch her neck while helping her with her coat or giving her a goodnight kiss on her cheek. If things are getting a little more intimate, brush over the area with soft lips, gentle nibbles and light touches with the tips of your fingers. She won't be able to handle much of this before passion takes over. Be prepared.

Surprise her

Make the setting romantic. Set out candles, fresh flowers and sensual snacks that will be suitable for intimate play later – like whipped cream, strawberries and creamy chocolate sauce. Her romantic mood can turn erotic – quickly.

Spice it up

She is highly sensual, and pleasant sensations involving taste, touch and texture will please her: the softness of silk against her body, warm oil gently rubbed over her chest, or a touch of honey enjoyed off her neck ... be creative.

Remember: Never push her into trying anything she's not keen on. She will expand her erotic horizons willingly – but at her own pace.

Her expectations

The magic touch. Although the Taurus female may be described as traditional and conservative in bed, she is far from boring. She doesn't need to reinvent traditional positions; she has her own way of making them very pleasurable.

Keep it comfortable. She's not into kinky stuff, and her fantasies tend to remain fantasies. She does, however, get a kick out of having sex in different places, including outside. But she has no delusions about sex on the beach in the moonlight, with grains of sand going everywhere. For her, sex needs to be comfortable, no matter where it happens. So make sure to bring a blanket!

A little tenderness. It's important to her to receive small gestures of affection when making love, like cuddles and kisses. She is not a demanding lover, but she will expect her partner to show initiative and passion. A quick one under the covers with the lights out will offend her.

Light her fire. Sex is important to her. Her sensual pleasures are often guided by her feelings, which is why she seeks deeper connections with sexual partners.

Embrace the moment. Her lover needs to pay close attention to her needs; she expects him to be just as passionate as she is.

Your sensual preferences
Quiz yourself and find out whether this woman is for you.

Where on the scale are you?
1 = Don't agree | 3 = Sure | 5 = Agree!

1. Experiencing each other through touch and taste increases sensual pleasure.
One a scale for 1 to 5, you are : 1 - 2 - 3- 4 - 5

2. There is no such thing as passionate sex without a comfortable setting.
One a scale for 1 to 5, you are : 1 - 2 - 3- 4 - 5

3. A constant need for erotic adventures can make you superficial and restless.
One a scale for 1 to 5, you are : 1 - 2 - 3- 4 - 5

4. Romantic feelings can make sex far more intense.
One a scale for 1 to 5, you are : 1 - 2 - 3- 4 - 5

Score.
15 - 20: Steamy, intense, passionate – and loving. Enjoy!
10 - 14: She may be a slow starter at times, but as soon as her interest is sparked, she'll make up for the delay.
05 - 09: She may require a bit more passion and intensity than you're used to. Give into her sensuality and explore new erotic depths.
01 - 04: Your preferences are completely different to hers. Flexibility and communication will be important to achieve a satisfying sex life.

CHAPTER 4

GENERAL STUFF

The big picture

Keep in mind that the characteristics of a Taurus may vary quite a bit depending on where within the sign she was born, as well as a wide range of additional astrological factors. But for now, let's stick to the basics. Just remember: don't jump to conclusions as soon as you meet her. Give her room to shine. Get to know the woman behind the sign.

Her personality: Pros and cons

Pros	Cons
• Generous	• Lazy
• Loyal	• Stubborn
• Friendly	• Materialistic
• Supportive	• Overindulgent
• Determined	• Slow starter
• Sensual and passionate	• Conservative
• Feminine and playful	• Reluctant to change
• Humorous	• Conventional
• Romantic	• Narrow-minded
• Productive	• Cautious
• Persistent	• Unimaginative
• Reliable	• Overly sentimental
• Genuine	• Unforgiving
• Self-disciplined	• Afraid of failure

Tip: How to show romantic interest

Little things will get you far.
Unexpected attention makes her
heart sing. Text her and let her know
you're thinking about her. Offer to
cook dinner or give her a backrub
when she's tired.

Romantic Vibes

Miss Taurus:
The loyal and romantic partner

The essence

The soft touch. Although she may come across as practical, organised and determined, her love life is completely different.

Make a move. She is used to being assertive in her professional life, which is why she prefers her man to take the initiative in her romantic life.

Masculinity and strength. A strong man makes her feel safe and supported. It's also very important that he desires her, both romantically and erotically.

Joy! She won't fill her days will exotic sex and unexpected surprises, but there will be loads of sensual pleasures, fun adventures and joy for her and her partner.

Embrace life. She believes that life is not only for living, but also for loving – and she embraces pleasures big and small. This philosophy is important to her. A man who doesn't appreciate the finer things in life will not be able to make her happy.

Tip: How to show erotic interest

Be sensual, with a warm voice and a seductive look in your eyes. Remember, she's not good with hints. Be direct but in subtle way. If she feels cornered by your passion, she'll turn away.

Erotic Vibrations

Miss Taurus:
The sensual and tender lover

The essence

Choosy. She won't throw herself at the first guy who looks in her direction. The Taurus woman is very choosy. But as soon as she has made up her mind about a man, she evolves into a goddess of sensual pleasures.

Sensual. She knows exactly how to get her lover in the mood by dressing seductively, speaking in a low, warm and sensual voice and making the surroundings as comfortable as possible.

Say yes! She has a strong sex drive. If you want to be her lover, you mustn't turn her down very often – or at all.

Keep your promises. If you have hinted at a sensual evening, the Taurus woman will play with the thought for hours and be excited when she sees you. If you end up working late, don't expect any sympathy when you finally arrive. The hot vibes will be gone. A cold shoulder is probably all you're going to get.

CHAPTER 5

COMPATIBILITY QUIZ

Are you banging your head against the wall, or does she unleash your positive potential? Do you provoke her or bring out the best in her? Is she making you throw your arms into the air in exasperation, or do you feel inspired and complete in her company? Take the test to find out.

Question 1.
Would you describe yourself as observant?

A. No. I can be extremely absentminded, and I often wander around in my own world.
B. Sometimes, if I smell a new perfume or something cooking, or anything vivid like that.
C. Yes. I pick up on hints easily.

Question 2.
Where would you prefer to have sex?

A. In a luxurious hotel room.
B. I'm not that particular. Any place is good enough for me.
C. In comfortable surroundings: a large, soft bed with soft music, candles, loads of cushions, a bottle of champagne...

(cont.)

Question 3.
When it comes to sex, what's most important?

A. Adventure and playfulness.
B. Passion and sensuality.
C. Not sure. Sex is no big deal.

Question 4.
If you were buying your partner a surprise gift, what would you go for?

A. I know she loves luxury ... maybe a nice pair of shoes or a cashmere sweater.
B. I'd keep it simple. Flowers – she'd love that.
C. Presents are for birthdays and Christmas!

Question 5.
Do you compliment your woman when you're out with friends?

A. Yes, of course I do. I'm very proud of her.
B. Not really. Either I forget – or can't find a reason to compliment her.
C. Sometimes, when it feels natural.

Question 6.
Is financial security important to you?

A. Piggybanks and savings accounts are not my style.
B. Yes – financial security means financial freedom.
C. I try, but I'm not all that great with budgets and spreadsheets.

Question 7.
Do you often make an effort to please your woman – in general?

A. Every now and then – provided I've got the time and feel up to it.
B. Of course I do; I love her!
C. I seldom find time for that.

Question 8.
How would you respond if your partner told you she had splashed out on a very expensive silk nightdress?

A. I would have told her off for being financially reckless. That's crazy!
B. Well, it's her money. She can do whatever she wants with it.
C. I enjoy having a seductive woman lying next to me in bed...

Question 9.
Do you expect your partner to play along every time you're in the mood?

A. No. Sometimes we're busy with other things and not focused on sex. It's normal.
B. Of course. When I want sex, I want it now!
C. Not really – even though I wish she would.

Question 10.
Do you think it's OK to enjoy weekend-type- treats – wine, special food, etc. – during the week?

A. No. It's important to distinguish between weekdays and the weekend.
B. Yes, of course. Every day is for living – not just Friday, Saturday and Sunday.
C. Sure, provided I can afford it.

SCORE	A	B	C
Question 1	1	5	10
Question 2	5	1	10
Question 3	5	10	1
Question 4	10	5	1
Question 5	10	1	5
Question 6	1	10	5
Question 7	5	10	1
Question 8	1	5	10
Question 9	10	1	5
Question 10	1	10	5

75 – 100

You probably feel like you've found the woman! She is strong, positive and confident, and she keeps your spirits high, no matter what happens. She wakes you up in the morning with a gentle kiss and a playful sparkle in her eyes. Your friends are probably envious. Keep treating her like a princess, and she'll do her best to live up to your expectations. Sometimes people just click. Why overthink it? Just enjoy and cherish it.

51 – 74

Life is wonderful. You have found a woman who satisfies and inspires you. Sure, you'll have a few heated discussions. But although you don't always agree, you respect each other's opinion. You are probably a little more sexually assertive than she is, but this could actually be an advantage for her – provided you don't push her. Pay careful attention to her moods. As you probably know, this woman doesn't wear her heart on her sleeve. When in doubt, ask her. And don't settle for a 'Oh, it's nothing'. If you communicate well, you will avoid silly misunderstandings. And one final note: Don't forget to compliment her whenever she has made an effort to please you.

26 – 50

Every now and then, you may wonder whether it's worth it. But if you really love her, you should give it a try. Barrelling forward with your fingers crossed won't do the trick. You'll need to make a concerted effort to understand each other. Is she acting slightly boring? This could be her way of showing you that she's unhappy with how things are. The worst you can do in a situation like this is to nag her. Yes, she can be stubborn. Although this may provoke you, try guiding her instead of pushing. You will be surprised to discover how much you can achieve if you approach conflicts with humour rather than anger. Show her your charming, sensual and tolerant self, and watch how she brightens up!

10 – 25

You might as well face it: this won't last long. A romantic relationship should be based on love, not practical arrangements. It may be time for both of you to explore the mysteries of love – elsewhere. You deserve something better, and so does she.

Suggestion

A quiz may give you a few hints, but life offers amazing and sometimes surprising nuances. If you make each other happy, then embrace the joy, cherish the love and explore the opportunities ahead!

...just a final note:
This book has not been approved by your date and should be treated accordingly. He or she *may* not agree with the content.

Made in the USA
Las Vegas, NV
05 December 2023

82143107R00046